C
by
Marcus Skjøte

Copyright © 2015 by Marcus S. Skjøte
All rights reserved. This book or any portion thereof
may not be reproduced or used in any manner whatsoever
without the express written permission of the publisher
except for the use of brief quotations in a book review.

ISBN: 978-1-326-23179-8
Copyright: Marcus Skjøte (Standard Copyright Licence)
Edition: First Edition.
Publisher: Marcus Skjøte
Published 29th March 2015
Front cover picture owned and used by author.

For the loved ones lost, and those not yet met.

Contents:

1 - Angelic disgrace
2 - An elegy to purity and faith
3 - The fall
4 - An elegy to gravity
5 - The headless statue
6 - An elegy to myth
7 - Kefka
8 - Truth
9 - Gravity
10 - The moon, the man and his heart
11 - Alskling
12 - Wolves
13 - Serenity be my heart
14 - Mansken and Solsken
15 - Time
16 - Little child
17 - A cliff edge
18 - Ghosts of adoration
19 - Bend my knee
20 - Thrones
21 - Betrayal
22 - Morning rise
23 - Stigmatize
24 - Verum
25 - Nullum Aequilibrium
26 - The sons of disobedience
27 - Protecting my devotion
28 - Like sand through fingers
29 - Land of followers
30 - The creator
31 - The sparrow
32 - The puppet
33 - The nest
34 - The garden of rose
35 - The snake
36 - Prison of mirrors

37 - Vict(or)im
38 - Empire and ashes
39 - Dirge
40 - The mask
41 - Friend but foe
42 - What seems
43 - From winter to spring
44 - Love's caress
45 - The kings of dirt
46 - Ends
47 - Tales
48 - What we ought
49 - The days are lost
50 - Rainy mourning
51 - Congregation
52 - Beauty
53 - Re-enacting the night
54 - Words as games
55 - Alone
56 - The reflection we create
57 - Throne of Atonement
58 - A day not come
59 - Ink of the past
60 - Past masters
61 - Age
62 - Prince
63 - The sovereign come
64 - Left
65 - Pigs and angels
66 - Contemplation's call
67 - Ignored importance
68 - Bleach
69 - Dipped in sin
70 - For whom tears aren't shed
71 - Mi amor
72 - Old towers
73 - Para tí

74 - The city
75 - The wheelchair
76 - To say
77 - When I compare to a rose
78 - Both as one
79 - Silence
80 - The realistic offer
81 - Crave
82 - The leprosy
83 - The hermit
84 - Cycle
85 - Type of man
86 - Empty house
87 - Marx of history
88 - Percy's romance
89 - Dreams be Dunn
90 - Eyes to see
91 - Anti-life
92 - The dog's bite
93 - Repeated lines
94 - That which is due
95 - The cold bed
96 - The face
97 - A stranger to me
98 - The serpent of light
99 - Ode to Wales
100 - The sin of solitude

1 - Angelic disgrace:

He stands from his throne,
Complete but always alone.
The dust mocks him, building with time.
His pride being his only crime.

The torn off crown cuts the face,
Of that pale angelic disgrace.
Unhearing, unseeing, woven into its place,
The heart beats until it turns to waste.

With the blood gushing from his face,
He muttered words with rhythmic pace;
"Do you feel the same as me,
The wild fire in all who see?
Unravelling forward my world's embrace,
Love with freedom to shine on one's grace.
Leaving forever all fears with glee,
Another, yet better me, will I be."

2 - An elegy to purity and faith:
There are two things expected of me,
To follow them, there is no reason I can see.
They are and always have been assumed virtuous,
But expecting without reason concludes them monstrous.
There are now no wreathed words,
To save me and clean away life's dirt.
Expose the wound and heal no hurt,
Purity: a concept, entirely absurd.
Will I heel like an obedient dog?
To he who that 'deserves' my praise: god?
Why demand of me faith?
When you reject of me your eternal face?

3 - The fall:
Attacking the heavens, the time has come.
While burning with rage, the end of my spear.
Advancing serpent's head, forcing my deity to appear.
Rebelling, a war that cannot be won.
You summon in me the sceptical frown.
The time beginning, or ending, is near.
Full of confidence, and yet so much fear,
I have come for your presence, I want to be shown.

Why is it: my deity, you don't come down?
To show me the face of your divinity.
To prove yourself, and me wrong?
I have waited for proof of you for so long,
You enthral yourself in mist: Obscurities'
King. Be gone or come and claim your crown.

4 - An elegy to gravity:
Not every man can prove their weight, their worth.
With dreams of wings I am forced to walk.
I wish to become the challenger of my own gravity,
To rise to a higher form of totality.
The wall that is the limit is metaphysical, ergo:
The size of my deed will reflect my ego.
Limitless being to our reality is an affront,
Project myself, I must become exactly what I want.
So gravity, I challenge you whilst I sing:
"I defy you to limit and crush my wings!"
In defiance I scream at my fate;
"I'll gain my wings and you'll keep your weight!"

5 - The headless statue:

A statue used to stand proud and tall,
From all around admiring eyes upon it did fall,
The sight: glamorous and leading the heart's of men,
Like lambs from grazing fields to the lion's den.

Time past is lost with yet more time,
History is forgotten and obscured by wrapped vine,
The statue's tale no longer sung,
And the God's bells no longer rung.

Cry to fill the man-made gaps,
Dragging you down with all that you believe,
Your mind and your heart deceived,
Chained corpse covered and hidden amongst the leaves.

Was the idol ever found?
Beheaded and missing his crown,
The Godhead has been removed,
The human heart no longer there to be abused.

I wasn't sure I could leave,
Evidently I was deceived,
Deep in my heart I sighed,
I took myself and left this time.

6 - An elegy to myth:
Wondrous tales told to enthral,
A drop of reality to wrap you in glorious shawl.
You listen intently to every word said,
Forgetting to live in this moment instead.
Wild and splendid archetypes to become,
Role models to guide what has now begun.
In your heart you feel your time is overdue.
Between God and man, myth and being, half which isn't you:
A path towards Godhead is directly defined,
But this path is too narrow for your mind:
Trapping and reducing you to a mere symbol,
Choosing to throw yourself to fate for the gamble.

7 - Kefka:[1]

Kefka Is my name,
Killing kings is my game
A mask to make me tame,
Now I'm out, never in again.

When people disagree with me,
I kill them with stamping, what a tragedy.
Lick the blood from my shoes,
Taste It like all the other fools.
Combing a desert for scum.
Becoming a God so I can kill everyone.

I hate everything but myself:
Because what's more beautiful than ones self?
You heard me the first time, Kefka Is my name,
And I'm trying to kill everything for fame.
Burning, rotting, death's embrace:
I promise you: You'll die crying looking at my jester face.

---

[1] Based on Kefka Palazzo.

8 - Truth:

Blood fed flower, beautiful yet so sour.
To wander with countless hours;
The sun rising spills grief with its rays,
There's always darkness to show the way.

It's hunger that opened my eyes to reality,
Indulgence in my desires and limited abilities.
This is perpetual, never ending;
Our freedom, we each our own gods of emptiness.

Mocking reality with the unfathomable perfect,
Nothing experienced or spoken is such a word.
Life itself, is the only gift given.
To hold truth in my arms, not perfection, is my happiness.

9 - Gravity:

Not every man can prove their weight, their worth.
With dreams of wings I am forced to walk.
I wish to become the challenger of my own gravity,
To rise so much higher than fate will allow.

A wall of fate; nothing satisfies.
Just because I defy you, doesn't make me wrong.
The size of my deed will reflect my ego,
Project myself, I must become exactly what I want.

So gravity, I challenge you to keep me down,
I defy you to crush my wings!
In defiance I scream at my fate;
"I'll gain my wings and you'll keep your weight!"

10 - The moon, the man and his heart:
I'm leaving.
I shall go forth to conquered and barren lands,
To find an object to perfectly mirror your beauty.
Alas I have only seen one thing worthy of that comparison,
The Moon on Its perfect monthly night,
I cannot capture nor give that to her, for I am just a man.
It's the only thing with comparable beauty to my Princess.
And If I could, I would present her with such a gift just for her.
My heart being the second gift to offer.

11 - Alskling:

I was dressed entirely in black,
And you...In yourself.
Perfect...I never knew such a thing...
And there you was, staring right at me.

Your eyes always told me what you couldn't say;
That you were mine and wished you could stay.
Your lips taught me everything,
But how to live without you.

And every night I dream of you,
You approach me and say what you couldn't.
Your lips touch mine,
Making me yours.

And I wake up, dressed In darkness,
Think of you dressed in yourself.
A beauty so true,
Not one has compared to you.

Every night I dream of you,
I tell you what I couldn't;
I adore you, I want you to stay.
To be able to hold you and take you away.

And I wake up, dressed In darkness.
Think of you dressed In yourself.
A beauty so true,
Not one has compared to you.

And every night I dream of you.
Wake up in depression from the lack of you.
And wonder If I had said, what I never said;
That I wanted you too.

And maybe if I had said...what I never said...
Would there be beauty In my arms when I wake Instead?

12 - Wolves:
Sick of the pack, the wolves.
Running and seeking while staying together,
Singularity Is none existent to you.
Strength in numbers, weakness In singles.

Throw your morals at my face,
When you're the one who forgot them.
I never swore loyalty to you,
And you have never shown me such a thing.
And yet I'm meant to be,
When I left you didn't even notice.
If I did stay would you know?

You can scream betrayal from your tower,
You can tell a story of my deeds.
Words are words and actions are real,
Saying something doesn't make It so.

With my actions I only grow,
With your words you'll have nothing to show.
When they forget their love for you,
You'll realize It was only pity.

13 - Serenity be my heart:
In the silence of the night:
Dressed In darkness, I approach my love.
I Whisper to soothe her heart;
"Long have I waited...Alone...For you"

In this secret place, we stand together.
In silence, we need nothing.
In this secret place, I want nothing.
Serenity is my heart, In the presence of my goddess.

14 - Mansken and Solsken:
Two sides of the same coin:
Completely different but inexplicably the same.
Only an edge to separate,
It's the celebrated line to mark differences and strengths.

Mirrors with different reflections and reflections showing different faces.
What is the edge to the world but a whimsical twist of fate?
What If a flip could unite and erase the edge?
And who's to say what fate would throw when an edge Is landed.

Is It fate,
Our faces,
Or our strengths and
Differences that bind us together?

No.
Gravity and fate can try to tame,
But It's by our choice
That we play this game.

15 - Time:

There's a fate which I'm on my way,
A grave with my name,
A dog to tame, memories to frame,
A date assigned to my name.
A partner to kiss, all my friends to miss,
Random people I will hate,
A family to reciprocate,
My own mind to dominate,
My Intellect to elevate.
All this life will be mine;
All I want is for you to share my time.

16 - Little child:
I stand in a field, as a child.
A simple flower, I hold in my palm,
A symbol of how easily something can be crushed or blown away.
Nurture this beauty and sigh away my pains.
A lotus, the soul of my love,
I hold in my hand.

As I contemplated these thoughts;
An Angel made itself known, walking in, with no halo or Holy Father.
Suddenly I felt insecure and stupid,
A boy in love with a flower.

It approached me and took my hands in its palms gently,
An angel maybe but a woman I was sure.
She possessed soft hands like small pieces of stroking silk,
Encasing my hands so they formed like fists.

A panic, I fell into fear as I began to crush my love, my flower.
Anxiety and pain, my heart began to cry and so did I:
She smiled and opened my hands palm up to show me,
The flower was still there and as perfect as uncrushed.

I awoke from this dream, a man.
I realized the flower was my love and my hands the rest of the world;
The hands are unable to crush what I love,
Love is something more, something untouchably strong.
As I studied my dream and its meaning,
I realized I was holding something in my arms:
The flower, the angel, the woman
And my love.

17 - A cliff edge:

Every night I drift into sleep;
The same dream, the same adventure each time.
For my mind is spiralling and trying to find:
What does any of this mean?

And I find myself now, half way through my life,
I've found a cliff edge.
Abyss will you eat me? Consume and take my pride?
I have found I'm alone.

I look into this abyss:
With no master I seem to recognize my own face,
With no slave I seem to see my fate.
I wish to become my master.
Time falls like grains of sand,
I think I've found the answer.

The sands come, the gap is my grave.
Right or left no longer open to choice,
For forward is my domain.
A path to Princedom is shown.

As I fall I realize my reward: Pain.
Rewards are always double edged.
Humanity a higher animal.
Yet deprived and depraved to the core.
Feed yourself.

I return as my master,
Not a son of any morning.
I am here to feed myself,
I return to reverse my deprivation,
To indulge my depravations.

18 - Ghosts of adoration:
Up until now, adoring what you haven't seen.
After today, it'll be as If you have never been.
They will cry for you, assuming sorrow for the loss;
In their hearts they long for you, jaded with anger at the cost.

Speak a soft eulogy.
The life spoken about much harsher.
This life was a cancer to you,
And faith: the reason.

Now he has died, with weeping angels does he stay.
I always came across seemingly lost within my way.
A mask to cover so I no longer have to stay.
Fate doesn't decree anything from me:
Living for passion, filling eternity.

19 - Bend my knee:

Living out savage days,
We find our path and discuss our ways.
People leave and pass me by,
And always I think of one.

Blessed with beauty,
Such as I had not.
You interest me beyond comprehension;
Staining the scent of my skin.

I bend my knee to just one,
Pledged myself in days I can't remember,
For her grace I am anything,
Thoughts of her...I feel like nothing.

20 - Thrones:
As I once took on your decree,
Agreed and was subjective to thee,
I honour myself with my revoke,
Of everything you once spoke.

Being led by something less than real,
Conjuring what I thought I should feel,
No man should rule another,
His King Throne for no other.

21 - Betrayal:

Is that the mouth that spews out lies?
Is that the cause of your demise?
The lowest point will always be the end,
When you're alone and have no one left to bend.

Cut a bond so I have less.
You're exactly like all the rest.
Betrayal: A murky game,
Showing you have no shame.

Trying to take what is mine.
You're a mirror,
And I don't have the time.
For all you say and do:
You prove yourself not to have a "You".

22 - Morning rise:
See that my pain is real.
That you know how I feel,
And I confess my loneliness,
In hope that you will feed me your tenderness.

I can sustain myself during the lonely nights,
Because your love lasts a lifetime.
I find myself holding onto that word that I so hate:
Hope.

The sun remains silent.
Everything changes,
But your benevolence.
Burn away the day,
Seek me In the night.
And just like the morning rise:
I rise and fall with the day.

And in great days yet to befall,
The sun shall embrace the moon
And in silence tell of its love.
With pride not measured by distance,
a heart not torn or rendered by greed:
I shall love you as my second half.

23 - Stigmatize:

And ever reliving that dark room,
you seated as if upon a throne.
I remember your words:
"Well done my son.
You have become
Intelligent, strong,
Independent! And worthy of pride!
Your reward is also your punishment:
Loneliness.
If you can make it so this doesn't stigmatize you...
You will be truly strong!"

I always thought my isolation was a weakness.
My loneliness a flaw, a thing to be shunned and ignored.
I now realize my unwillingness
And lack of social want is what I am.
My difference, my isolation:
Makes me strong.
It has become a matter of pride
That I don't interact with what I don't need.

24 - Verum:

Oh angel of Verum,
Your truth is the lion's sword.
Solomon is calling:
Pride in your vanity.
My great apterous one,
In no eyes have you fallen.
You're adorned with the
Paleness of celestial beauty.

And behind your back, I praise your deeds.
Fill this temple with blood;
I'll drown in glory not worship.
A symbol like a halo around your neck.

I live for the day this play will end,
So I can remove my mask.
Tell the story of my heart and pride,
Until then my face I hide.

25 - Nullum Aequilibrium:
Not one step back.
Eyes locked forward.
Necks built to break,
Empires to fall.

I've tried your philosophy, It doesn't work for me.
To be pushed around and keep your sweetness,
All the helping hands will fade away,
As you have no will to stand.
So tired of the lack of everything I desire,
All to be told "You're nothing to me."

Are they all weak,
Rude, stupid and slanderous?
All of your pathetic deeds...
Make them remember.

Show the weak man the truly strong,
He will try to mirror his strengths.
So fragile, so easy to break;
In the broken shards I see your face.

Wrap yourself in lies,
How you wish them to be true.
Strength is being able to live with lies,
Not a single second spent believing them.

I live in this world of subjective truths,
Not for a moment do I fall.
I see your weakness...
And I'll make you remember.

26 - The sons of disobedience:
The eyes of the devil,
Synchronized with the night.
Dance yourself unto me,
Dance so beautifully.

Eternally,
Under the power of me.
Slave shall have a master;
On your knees forever after.

A skin of mockery.
Deprivations: no need to be tame.
Call me by my name
When you're festering in shame.

As it was,
And as it is;
On the ashes of the fallen,
Won't you dance with me?

You mock yourself in dance.
Love is forever your trance.
So dance on the ashes of the dead,
Show me the beauty inside your head.

Come, rejoice and join us:
The Sons of disobedience.
Revel in our name,
We have no time or place for shame.

27 - Protecting my devotion:

Let my all judging eyes turn on themselves
So I may see my imperfections.
Devour the parts that I despise with the teeth that have
Without mercy destroyed so many before me.

It is so easy to criticize, rather than praise.
To destroy what you love with good intentions.
People always say you learn to appreciate
Something when you no longer have it;
I never was ungrateful, unappreciative of what I love.
The fear of loss fuels the fires of appreciation.

I'll be the ghost,
The guiding hand,
The scream when you can only whisper.
The bad days happiness,
The sun to your moon,
The light to your darkness,
The edge to your blade.

Because the most damaged of souls are those who protect
And heal those around them.
They have learnt through experience and error the pain of life.
With the empathy to see and feel the pain in your eyes,
That person becomes the protector and adorer of your virtues;
The breaker of your vices and the beating of your heart.
The moon to your sun,
The reflection of your love.

28 - Like sand through fingers:
I've dwelt with garbage, mockery and sickness became me.
I no longer wish to walk these sewers, cluttered gutters.
Trash will act as trash, no changing these people.
It's time to leave, be dignified and free.

It's hard to find yourself when you're covered in shit.
People grab and claw at me, I don't know why.
Life's like that, a fury of hands.
I snap these fingers now; poison lies!

Bless this new thing when truth washes over me.
When poison is lost and healing is found.
When you see your forbidden face,
Relive the past and see I deserve nothing from you.

And my existence will leave little trace on the world,
Because I am of little relevance.
Is that freedom or a curse?
My life is assumption and perpetual audacity.

And to this day I do not remember
When I offered myself away from the sun.
As the night comes to take me away,
Blood;
The gift of life is given.
...I no longer care for my destiny.

29 - Land of followers:
This land of followers;
Broken like water starved earth,
Cracked and opened by desolation.
More sun, more shadow
But never the healing rain.
And upon this land
You find me weak and uncrowned.

The throat was cut in the abyss of my dreams.
My hope poured forth like rivers
Away from me to starve me again.
Dethroned my crimson during this night,
The confessor of all of my deeds.

Knives and candles.
Fallen leaves and exhaled breaths.
Darkness and sheddings.
For now, I serve my purpose.
For now, I spill my grief.

And in that forest I found something within myself;
The path that took me to a lesson.
Take my heart and spit it into my eyes.
For I can no longer see
While clouded in tragedy.

The right of the evil man decree:
He shall have his heart broken but once.
The path of the good man taught me:
He shall have it broken daily.

30 - The creator:
This man, a creator, was happy alone.
Not socially inept but always working at home.
Remarkable man who made life size puppets.
Of every human likeness for a few ducats.

One day he made his finest work yet:
The most feminine and beautiful of the set.
This puppet was perfect to his eye.
He looked upon his work with a happy sigh.

The genius began to praise his work himself.
The puppet attracting admiration all by itself.
As often the brain compliments its own work.
Blind and never giving itself credit, is it's curse.

31 - The sparrow:

One day, the man took himself for a walk.
A sudden screeching sound halted him from his thought.
He found a crippled and dying Sparrow,
His heart and face was overcome with grief and sorrow .

Solemnly taking it in his hands:
This little bird of Sparrow died without a sound.
Took the body to his place of work,
To bury that beautiful and now decaying bird.

Upon his return a thought struck him profound,
That fatefully this Sparrow he had found,
As if by pure instinct he seized it's heart,
Placing inside the puppet, life to start.

It spoke with his voice of what it had seen:
"That glint in your eye, admiration, what does that mean?"
He replied a little delayed from surprise:
"Vanity in my work, or love, maybe, I surmise."

32 - The puppet:

Day by day, he taught it more,
Never did teaching his creation become a bore,
It was more person by each day,
Like a child, sponging information along the way.

He came to feel love for such a soul,
Paternal love nurturing, forming his role,
Slowly turning into something more,
Feelings growing inside, like nothing before.

The creator, father, teacher, lover?
Why was this one so distinct from the other?
Like the man who both loves and hates his wife,
Confusing, unable to clarify and clear his strife.

Without a thought he began to speak,
While submissively staring at his feet,
"Why can I not love you, what is so wrong with that?
Is it not true when the heart speaks, it speaks fact?"
The puppet fell silent and refused to reply,
He thought to himself "I'll know in due time."

33 - The nest:

Taking a walk to try and clear his mind,
Thinking with his feet and wasting a little time,
He heard chirping and felt somewhat better,
Around the next corner his final endeavour.

He found the puppet sat as if in rest,
With the heart removed from its chest,
He looked upon the chirping birds nest,
And knew this choice was for the best

He took the chicks and raised them good,
Did the best any mother Sparrow could,
He took them to a field one day,
Thus setting them free to fly away.

No longer making what he once loved,
He was more content to watch the doves fly above,
In his final days he came to realize,
That biological love is both truthful and wise.

34 - The garden of Rose:
Young lady once of my heart,
Now is your time to depart,
To grow and wander far apart,
Thus beginning the end of the start.

My ribs were spread apart,
Forced your way into my heart,
Bleeding red tears from the pain,
Falling like July's rain, who is to blame?

The white skin I bit in,
Like a wine yearning to be refined,
Merging pain with love,
Became my hate to cage the dove.

Amoureux, the only one,
Alone and almost gone,
Unable to atone,
I set her name in stone.

Rose garden burns to give me life,
To fuel nightmares where I mock that sacred rite,
When I awake from my sleep,
No tears do I weep.

Now: Drowning you in a pool of blood,
Your face encased in mud,
Every day the same dream,
Choking you in an ocean of blood.

Let the water enters your lungs,
Let the blood exit your eyes,
This is the taste...the image...the delusion,
Of revenge.

Wake with clean hand
With missing space in bed,
A searing pain destroying my head,
A heart that has killed its love instead.

And so I renter the sea,
Lye on my back and think,
Love the chain that led me to hate,
In my dreams you suffocate,
Trapped for all time,
Between my hate and heart.

On the dead love of a mother,
On the fallen pride of a father,
Lost all you had,
In the blink of an eye.

This covenant of vampirism,
You cannot drink your own blood,
With sword in hand,
These bonds will end.

And when this is all over and done,
My heart you would of surely re-won,
Place a thorn on my grave,
To signal your atonement is finally made.

35 - The snake:

Lately I have been slithering for you,
I would feel death for you,
But not live for myself,
Why should I forgive anything of you?

And you, who promises a body to such distance,
I taste distain,
And you, who promises a heart so hollow,
I will not fill you up.

I was always silent,
I always held my tongue:
I'm not waiting for any of you,
Dereliction Is not for me, I will not be left behind.

Look me in my eyes,
Stare at the face of your death,
Idiots bathed in greed,
Reap your fields of bullshit to believe In.

Because memories fade,
Underneath my scared skin,
Its anticipation I bathe In,
Because people fade...

I fell into nothingness,
Life Is but a dream,
And with each passing beat,
My heart is my own again.

Scorned, its wings taken,
Slithering, so long, so broken,
Burns it's tongue on the soaring Sun,
Until another day, another person come.

36 - Prison of mirrors:

With time I have come to ask the question why,
Solitude, loneliness, privacy and yet one more lie,
Unable to see into your heart and mind,
The revelation, the simplest of facts.

I see now, everyone justifies what they have done,
A noble cause to cover the true intent,
My eyes and heart burn from the facts,
I feel so lost and unable to act.

Now: Tell me why?
You cover yourself with justifiable lies,
I see nothing but your twisted face,
And feel only disgrace.

With these simply facts,
I no longer want to be a part of you,
I want to be free,
But these mirrored faces are mocking me.

And with time I might be able to re-blind my eyes,
To fall again for your simple lies,
With no eyes my heart will still scream,
Why do this with our lives?

Smash the mirror.
Deny the reflection.

37 - Vict(or)im:

Eyes open doesn't mean they see,
Mouth speaking doesn't have anything to say,
Finger pointing better off inverting itself,
You only see what you want.

And to this world I hold up my cup,
Sip and taste deprecation,
Happy at this distance,
Over which you drop your tears,
And you'll go on living in belief,
That tragedy was forced by your past years.

Credulous is your desire to victimize yourself,
Indifferent now to how you think and feel,
And the tragedy is that I no longer see,
How and why you seek to destroy me.

Drop by drop, stone by stone,
Destroy or create, our nature is known,
Weak and bathed in your fate,
Tell me again how you don't deserve my hate.

With a simple change,
Our lives and thoughts rearrange,
With a little time,
I have seen the justice in my rage.

Oh tell me, angel, and goddess, what has begun?
Why can't we stay forever?
All friends and love is gone,
Alone I face what I have done.

Life and death, incessant droning on we go,
Am I with you, in body? And spirit? Or mind?
Sing the praise of being together,
Sing on, Sing on and on and on.

38 - Empires and ashes:
Ashes of the old,
Flow through the new,
A crown to be found,
A king to be made.

Inherit this night,
Darkness be your weapon,
Guile be your second,
God? I: All I need.

Your empire,
Your legacy,
Mark me by this night,
Mark us with my rite.

No man is my brother,
I'll stand alone,
Blessed with the night,
On my pride, my deeds will reflect my ego,
On myself, I'll show you what I am.

39 - Dirge:

As I think of those old days,
I forget my current ways,
Before I speak I would like you to think,
What is pride to the dead?

Needing no object to bear our love,
No thoughts or ponderings of you above,
For if I knew where you now stay,
I know I would be fast to abandon my way.

So tell me how you know he is here,
How every little sign reduces your fear,
That he somehow watches and feels pride in us now,
Because I know deep down there is nothing left.

So I think back to those happy days,
When me and you were set in our ways,
So tell me how his heart swells with pride,
When he sees me with his none existent eyes.

My heart and memory are laced with you,
I am reminded by everything I do,
That the dead live on in our heart and mind,
Dirge to express my grief until you I re-find.

40 - The mask:

"Hail My ladies return!
I can hold her to my chest once more!
Hold up with pride this woman of all my affections,
Cast the mask of loneliness to the floor for now I wear my true face:
Happiness.

Stand next to me in silent contentedness,
For this true young lady is my Goddess
This Goddess is you!

"An angel without wings,
Of beauty and paleness the moon has crowned,
Opened my heart and hands to your throne,
And together we shall walk through the world."

And alone I think of those past words I said,
Alone I brave this world now through winds of demise,
Walking now, cloaked and protected from the Sun,
Solitary:
I walk my path with a mask of ugliness
Covering my once fair face.

41 - Friend but foe:

Once great king doth stand on his castle wall,
I am this man, now in pain awaiting his fall,
Awaiting his fate and loss of throne,
Fare rides on a horse for me to atone.

Give luck and progress to my foe,
So each new day brings a new challenge,
With each new rise I'm pained with their success,
I Fortuned my foe, and brought me only woe

How my tears have wetted this land,
How my scorn has blazed these people,
Fortune thus traveling down this blade,
My foe, once a friend in past unmade.

Great and splendid you stand before me,
Friend, oh how you have become my foe,
Tears and pain, taken and tamed,
My deeds, now shamed, not to be renewed again.

"My last words, my once close friend,
Before you put me to the blade,
I have but one thing to say,
Don't pray for fortune to bestow,
For fear of friend maketh him foe."

"My fortuned foe, how you frown at me,
I have once again brought you pain
Stole your love once before,
With my death I steal it once again."

42 - What seems:

Tell me your story little man.
Of your heart revealed like Sun.
How the light breaks through the trees.
How you've forgotten your once scraped knees.

No longer a child handicapped by sin.
More concerned with what's within.
You have grown up into a man.
From no obstacle have you run.

Within the heart of all proud men.
Lies a shard and the question 'When?'
Because when we grow up it seems,
Death becomes closer than our dreams.

43 - From Winter to Spring:
When winter is long gone,
I'll return in a few more,
Maybe then spring will regrow our barren lands,
For now It is too late.

Frozen tears on the face of a corpse,
Hide in your coffin,
Nailed shut like your eyes,
Is it fear that stays your hand from emergence?

But what use are you now?
Faith in nothing but my perplexion,
Bear with me for today,
And tomorrow you'll be repaid for your weariness.

And what are you God of anyway?
But the gravitation of my tears.
Bear with me tomorrow,
And wipe away your loneliness.

44 - Love's caress:
Love's caress,
Is affection undressed.
Hate confessed,
Is product of distress.

Holding to my chest,
An adoration felt at best.
She lies within my heart,
I confess she Is a part.

45 - The kings of dirt:

Blood drained from the body,
Eyes closing with ignorance,
Skin broken by the tests of life,
Whatever was promised, you gave only time.

The punishment given to this decrepit corpse,
Yet life remains, for the pride of another,
But gasping and ever losing,
Now eyes sealed shut with the weight of life.

You live like a shadow,
Unmoving and unthinking,
But yet you still speak,
Empty words with no thought for another,
The eyes shut but not the mouth,
Still passing on your poison words for a brother.

The corpse does still speak,
Words dripping with hatred that reek,
People with their credulity,
You they seek.

Rise ignorance and take your place,
Make a collective and erase your disgrace,
For now you sit upon your indignant throne,
With every sin in your mouth and no heart to atone.

Crowns falling like the sky on your days,
Power intoxicating, no change of ways,
You mock, you have lost your philosophy's,
Twisting down, modesty into hostilities.

Time will pass and so will your unmoving mind,
Then another ignorant bred king will shine.

46 - Ends:

Thinking back, I have no words to say,
I prefer to live and think within this day,
And I'm not really sure where I will go,
Or how, or why, or what fate will throw.

And today, only silence,
No longer living with yesterday's violence,
Don't speak, don't tell me, don't say how you feel,
Because no longer me, will I reveal.

Say farewell to that ghost lingering in your heart,
Because tonight and forever more we depart,
Flickering in the wind like a damaged flower,
Your hold, your grasp, on me you have lost your power.

47 - Tales:
Wondrous tales used to enthral,
With a speck of reality so you don't notice at all,
You listen intently to every word said,
Forgetting to live in this moment instead.

Archetypes to live up to,
Role models to guide what you become,
Deep in your heart you feel that your time is overdue,
Between God and man, myth and being, you're torn.

A path towards Godhead is often defined,
But this path is too narrow for your mind,
Trapping and reducing you to a mere symbol,
Choosing to throw your fate for the gamble.

48 - What we ought:
Truth in our eyes,
Subjective objectively blinds us with lies,
What is and what is not,
Rarely tells us anything of what we have got.

We need a system, a way,
That doesn't rely on what popularity does say,
Liquidize all known groups,
To make one social soup.

With no collective thought,
All singular, with truth as our ought,
We work together, not a equal,
I as we, and we as I,
Being as beings,
Singularly together.

49 - The days are lost:

You're not perfect,
And neither are you a miracle,
But you are not just another one,
Another angel to hide my sadness in.

Underneath the moon,
The wind asks me why,
Why do you wait?
And who do you wait for?

You're not perfect,
You're just another person,
Not blinded by Goddess' anymore,
But you feel like some kind of miracle.

I stand underneath the moon yet again,
I ask her who she waits for.
Why does she wait?
For the sun is her constant reply.

So another day,
I stand looking upon myself and ask,
Why do you wait?
For the moon, the face of pale beauty,
But that is not why,
I have no reply,
And still another day,
Spent beneath the moon.

All days link,
Stars moving and me underneath,
With the stoic placid face,
I stare unmoved by the beauty.
Waiting...

50 - Rainy mourning:

Twisting, turning,
Sighing and yearning,
Staring, eyes burning,
Beneath the flame, a tear.

Standing in front of stone,
Cold, stained and crumbling,
Standing in front of your legacy,
Not a word, but grieving.

Broken ties and lost brothers,
The day doesn't stop and now does my heart,
Rain falling, weight on my shoulders,
I still remember that letter and number.

Kneeling in front of a stone,
Cold to the touch and crumbling away,
Kneeling in front of your epitaph,
Silent words, asking where you have gone.

Black days, cloud out the sun's rays,
Once a year I remember,
Rainy morning for mourning,
Standing and walking back into the world of men.

I whisper to myself:
"Your words unforgotten, and my stupid ones never forgiven.
And yet I still stand and live.
With your face my reflection mocks me with each day.
To pass on your legacy...
And this pain I'll soon forget."

51 - Congregation:

Strong, standing among the weak,
You showed them a way to their knees,
Empty but productive for you,
Relabeling the old as new.

The congregation of the Elite,
Standing tall on your feet,
Watching the weak grovel on their knees
Tell me again you do not deceive.

Mocking, praying, remembering the days,
Those where you didn't worry about your ways,
A Shepard of wolves,
Built your flock to take your fall.

The separation of the Elite,
No longer standing on your feet,
Grovelling on your pure knees,
Tell me again what it is you believe.

The trap, you pray,
You have fell for your own way,
Weak and lead astray,
When the wolf becomes the sheep.

52 - Beauty:

Born with the right of masters,
Ashes of the past blown from the urn,
Born with perfect symmetry,
Bow before the Gods of flesh.

This power tugs your fate,
Bestowed with perfect grace,
Spotless, beautiful face,
Burning the ugliest of our race.

Your clear and perfect eyes cannot see the future,
Beauty bestow not intellect nor till the pasture,
Time and sands that fall, take away,
You cannot still deaths call, decay today.

Locked within, not a blemish upon this skin
Delicate hands, future day withered and thin,
The softest, bluest eyes to disguise,
Silver tongue twists to snap out your lies.

Bitter, curdling with scorn
Beauty yet to lose its thorn,
Soothe hatred with your enemies demise,
Only for perfection, your eyes cry.

53 - Re-enacting the night:
With the darkest hair against the olive tanned skin,
The sweet angled face of that true grin,
Unravels like a man descending into sin,
With that the story doth only begin.

She smiled with teeth white seen through the night,
Over head we could hear something at flight,
There was something inside her, some kind of inner might,
Yet no fear held me like the way her beauty did tight.

Wrapped and inflamed by her hearts candescence,
I was unable to identify her beauties essence,
Nothing of this moment made any sense,
Both willing, both staying, neither shy, neither innocent.

Every beautiful moment is destined to fade and die,
But from that moment there was no disguise,
Forever everyday re-enacting this night in our way,
From each other do we never stray.

54 - Words as games:
I spoke my words with such wrath,
Like flames had ignited my laugh.
To the man across from me,
He now sat and shifted uncomfortably.

In arguments, trials and time,
Anger can create much crime.
But you sit and speak tenderly.
Alas, I can't take you seriously.

Underestimating the calmly stock,
Those stoic like a rock.
And when one speaks too soft for me,
I will stop and inspect your audacity.

So when in argument commit no foul,
But don't forget your critical scowl.
Because when a man speaks so tenderly,
He often manipulates what you can see.

55 - Alone:

Writing my heart on this page below.
Hoping my words are able to flow.
From one person to another.
For kindness isn't restricted to the lover.

I can't ask anyone to return me home.
Surrounded by others but yet feeling alone.
Yes, even our sweetest promises can sour.
Long past will come our love's hour.

Don't forgive me for my conclusion,
No longer willingly protect myself with delusion.
Loneliness is not a thing unfelt by the strong,
But a slow flowing poison that takes far too long.

Don't ask me "Who is the one?"
For my days are early and barely begun.
Every morning can welcome you with a kiss.
You don't need to belong to anyone to feel like this.

56 - The reflection we create:

From water and warmth does life come.
Mass of infinite energy is how it all begun.
Mountains erupt from the sea which organisms can now flee.
Determining the path of forms, separating land, air and sea.

Bloodshed, the smashing of skulls.
Eons past which history cannot recall the deeds of all.
Slowly, agonizing steps towards our current state.
Community becoming a new necessity to our fate.

An idea, a concept being carried inside the brain.
While all the time our violence being tamed.
Seeing our reflection for millennia's past.
With no language to express our contrast.

Finally like a baby speaking its first lame words.
Forming sentences and developing our verbs.
Making crude sketching's and becoming more social.
The benefit to us more and more crucial.

With effort comes the self-expression.
Which with time reduces our stress.
Rhyming and enjoying our speech, conversing in verse.
Yet still flawed and carrying an old ancient curse.

Still quite evidently a branch of the ape.
Murdering, abusing and indulging in rape.
As the language progresses the self-expression takes a turn.
We create symbols of our self, those who reject them: They burn

With this our life took an ironic fate.
Like an artist who shows his talent with paint.
He made something beautiful, and then praised his art.
Forgetting he was the creator from the start.

Many millennia past and this painting still isn't lost.
The concept of God, what has that cost?
Angels fall from the sky to signal the end time has come.
Or has the ape been deluded by his own face since time began?

57 - Throne of Atonement:

I find myself leaving nothing but space with time.
I find myself with no light of my own to shine.
Working hard to gain reason for pride.
Digging out and finding nothing inside.

Alone or lonely? To belong to myself only.
Caged or free? Doesn't matter much to me.
You love now but later will only feel shame.
For having no power over a heart you wanted to tame.

With your wool dyed black.
You have no hope of turning back.
Do you think anyone would care?
If you vanished into thin air?

Denying the legion, committing family treason.
Breaking the ties and losing the value assigned to you with their eyes.
Is it a crime to cut your own tree down?
And to melt down that tarnished old crown?

Looking for guidance, not in my credence.
In myself only, seeking to make self-reliance.
Leaving the dust to rule my abandoned throne.
Sin? Disobedience? No urge to atone.

No longer stained with the names of fathers.
No longer in the affectionate hands of our mothers.
Willing to treat with equality as if like brothers.
There's no telling what we have left to discover.

58 - A day not come:

Maybe one day I'll be closer to the source.
Maybe one day I'll find the words.
But don't bet on it.
Don't bet on me.

As corrupted as all the rest.
Ill as any, with pale grey flesh.
It's not pessimism or lack of ego.
But being realistic and knowing your limits.

There will always remain the bitter core.
Born into a grave the past has bore.
I'm not looking for a way to money or fame.
Just a memory to reclaim and frame.

So don't look to me for advice.
I am just as confused as you.
Trying to live openly but always hiding.
There is always something we forget to say.

So maybe one day I will have the words.
But today is not that day.
I continue to live as lost as you.
Alone as you but you will never know.

Words are spoken for the few.
Nothing calls or beckons you.
Fate, an excuse to wait for nothing.
Move, walk, go, leave and live for you.

59 - Ink of the past:

There's a place I meet the broken dreams of those past.
On the way dried foot prints found upon the dirt path.
There, people come and go, frown and groan, not a place for the crass.
Honouring those still loved who during life couldn't last.

The sun and night may daily pass.
Along with the growing and cutting of the grass.
These remains remain and will always have no life left.
But that doesn't stop the heartbreak in people's chest.

Engraved with words from those that still love.
Hoping that what they feel is seen from above.
Walking back through that dried mud path.
Our present never escaping our sorrow filled past.

Little ornaments and significant novelties cover the graves.
From tormented hearts, the gifts they once received or gave.
We all know that death is not something to be tamed.
So we write on, adding to our beautiful yet tragic tome.

On and on another page,
Recollecting those forgotten days.
When we write, we write from past.
With our life's ink, that will forever last.

60 - Past masters:
Conquering grounds, delivering them into unseen hands,
Taking, as the swords are shimmering,
Stamping towards another new found land.

Immaculate, not a stronger power to be found,
Rising, this new state glimmering,
Marching forward, raze to the ground.

We take, So obey your new master,
Defiled, the spilled blood shimmering,
Taken towns have no history forever after.

Escaping past masters, struggling towards disaster,
Hope, the eye of the state still glimmering
Walking forward ever faster.

This empire all falls down,
Once had the whole world trembling,
No longer makes the power hungry moan.

Our state, now left alone,
On us the sun no longer glimmering,
Now dust sits on our throne,
Glory, has stopped shimmering,
For our violent past, we wish to atone.

61 - Age:
No grey,
Living with haste,
Youthful serene happy grace.
Walking excitedly towards each day
Joy of closed eyes,
Short lived happiness,
Becoming adult.

Clenched teeth,
The stress increased,
Finding your own path.
A talent to make yours
With things to gain,
Sowing your grain
Pride-worthy mane.

Long days,
Drawn out waste,
Ever towards death's embrace.
When the body walks to
The grave of deception,
Incinerated in subjection,
Solitary rejection.

Darkness embrace,
Imprisoned and encased,
My body to take.
Nothingness is a solitary path
With no footsteps
I leave only,
A grave.

62 - Prince:

Goodnight sweet prince,
For words and feelings mince,
The world values you no more,
Than love unleashed from fate's craw.

Close your eyes and fade away,
Like winter come into summer's day,
Leave the world to its own decay,
You were not meant to stay.

So leave this behind to the few,
It was always better me than you,
I am this prince to eternity play,
I'm bitter and I've lost my way.

So whisper sweetly into my ear:
"Goodnight, sweet Prince, I'll be here."
Tell me you love me and wish I could stay.
On that fateful, bitter, winter's day.

So cold, so fragile.
Not long to stay.
Leaving this world now I decay.
"Good morning, sweet Prince" I'll not hear today.

63 - The sovereign come:
In the time of the sovereign,
Freedom is self-produced.
You stand alone while the many stay confused.
When you let go of your pathetic past philosophies.
We contest with conflict to approve of you.

Waiting, spiralling, the judgement from your eyes.
Feeling, seeking, the time of sovereign nears.
All the weaknesses emerge from the ocean of deception.
Sinking, drowning in this new found perception.

In this moment of your sovereignty.
Ignoring assumptions based on divinity.
Are you burdened by the name of a father?
No longer grovel in view of another.

The sovereignty is you.
Your freedom is overdue.
Demanding you for yourself.
Self-reflection leads to wisdom's wealth.

64 - Left:

Too many days wasted on your solemn ways.
Unable to feel joy, using people as toys.
Preying on the tenderness of others,
But never doing anything to help another.

So I left you alone, we all left you alone.
You cry at the injustice, when justice has been given.
You moan at the solitude, when you have earned nothing else.
So we leave you alone, and you'll stay alone.

<u>65 - Pigs and angels:</u>
The shiny hangs vertical in strips of oink's torn out flesh,
But none have the same salty aroma.

Shaped like the disc upon heads;
Which sits horizontally on the pale skinned,
Genderless creatures of old paintings and glasses.

66 - Contemplation's call:
Contemplation of all That has gone before.
Solitude to find Yourself is poetry's law.
Finding the voice,
That says: "I must."

Spiralling into that state again.
Looking for that old, familiar resolve.
I came back, I always come back.
For a purpose, For a cause.

Closing eyes but brightening the light.
I find with solitude, I am not alone.
We all share together,
This contemplation to which we are thrown.

I return to you like a child,
Searching for embracing arms.
Those arms are mine,
Longer and more tender with time.

67 - Ignored importance:
Stable and sturdy.
Standing secure.
Solidly strong.
Solitary but never alone.

Sands have shifted to empty the glass.
I don't notice you or the time that has passed.
I pour my love and solitude onto you,
And my passions are inscribed into your skin.

Torn out pages resting next to arcane books.
Light scratchings and the ink stained palm.
I rest at you,
I enrage on you.
My deepest thoughts and sincerest pains
Lay scattered on your back.

68 - Bleach:

The wind blowing leaves and grass over this green place,
Like a new-born baby's hand gliding across its parent's face.
The trees bending towards their sides,
Almost blown over to the floor.
Like suffering cold fingers unable to stretch out of their claw.

Night taking from the day rays stealing.
I know the feeling,
Nights with hands held towards the ceiling.
I know this feeling,
I'm fully aware of my ties.
Like eyes seeking out but becoming lost in the skies.

In these nights the same question is asked of myself;
Am I like all of the rest?
Sharing not the name of father's,
But the home of others.
Related by distance,
Living beyond loved one's death.

Those white, bleached walls have a sound of their own.
Muffled by machines with tubes snaking to your bed throne.
The smell of suffering and anxiety was there,
Overwhelmed me but shed not a single tear.

I stood and smiled like a child:
"I'll see you when I get back."
It's not that I lacked the love to say:
"I want to hold your hand and wish to stay."

A month passed, that day of my return.
There was nothing to come back to,
Yet I did, to miss you.
You sleep in the night,
Yet the waters of life still flow.
Poisoned and black the river ebb and sway,
Running into my legacy to which I turn away.

My answer is yes,
I am like all the rest.

Wishing to sacrifice anything,
For a chance to alter what had gone before.
My desires are selfish and vain,
Return the love that soothed my pain.

69 - Dipped in sin:

Born sickly and weak,
For time and vanity's defeat.
Silence; because words offer no retreat.
Clinging, like a child to a protective sheet.

Broken and cracked the sensitive skin,
Dipped in liquid, dripping like sin.
From off me oozed the passionate hate,
Subjected always to the substance I hate.

Decrepit and pale,
A smile; a grin the veil.
Not a sound, not a single wail.
Self-fulfilling; destined to fail.

There were no words for me to speak,
But one thousand things to make me weak.
Mortality, in a soft pale shell.
Morbidity, suffering and constantly unwell.

Slowly and gradually learning to speak,
Always preferring to stay inside my head and think.
Scolded for miss-speaking,
From every word bitterness came to seep.

Silver was infused into my tongue,
For anyone who doubted I was strong.
Whipping others with my words,
To hide my own hurt.

Now the tongue is taken,
Whips the flesh of its maker
Can it break the skin of the one it's in?
Fighting a battle it knows it cannot win.

70 - For whom tears aren't shed:
Here they sit for a short while.
Lost in their own endless mind's trail.
And beneath the seat and dirt;
The past lies turned away from hurt.

Patches trodden hard and soft,
Deeds undone and words now lost.
In the past they rest for none to see
Unaware they sit, of life's tragedy.

Being so stuck in mind,
Ignorant of passing time.
What would they find if they dug this ground?
But just the over whelming, silencing sound.

They no longer sit, one by one.
All are taken, every one.
To pass another day,
While joined in grave,
To rest among the clay,
To turn their face away.

71 - Mi amor:
Come to me my little lady,
I promise to hold you near.
Come into my arms mi amor,
To form a love with only lack of fear.

You will get my sweetest and softest words in whispers.
Your little voice will always be heard;
As I hold you close enough in my arms;
That I can always hear you.

I will hold you in my arms,
Be wrapped around you with my mouth resting close to your ear,
To tickle it with my breath and whispered voice;
My lips only whisper soft and sweet words of love

72 - Old towers:
Derelict are the towers,
Spiralling and burying below,
Pushing always and ever down,
Through the depths of desire.

You're a machine,
An abandoned church,
Empty and lost,
Incomplete and failing.

I have the sharpest teeth you have felt,
And the silveriest tongue to whip you,
Destruction comes in all forms,
Words will be your delusions fall.

So I speak again,
Taking and raping,
I'll leave you empty.
Because it's how we all start.

In the hour of your corruption,
We assault you with judgment.
You're indulging in what is apparent,
While remaining entirely transparent.

Ignoring every lesson past,
Proving that you're useless trash,
Lessons are drilled in with pain,
Always acting alone in your self-made rain,
Try to tame and break others,
While the problem is your brain.

73 - Para tí:[2]

Tengo algo para tí:
Mi corazón y alma
Para calentar tu vida.
Mis labios,
Para tí mi amora;
Sólo tuyos.

Tu amor es más dulce;
Cuando cerca.
Y más amargo;
Cuando está lejos
Y soy todo tuyo;
Todos y cada uno de tus
Días y noches.

Yo si que te adoro,
Yo si que te amo,
Yo te quiero y deseo,

---

[2] **For you:**
I have something for you:
My heart and soul,
To heat your life.
My Lips,
For you my love;
Only yours.

Your love is sweeter;
When nearby.
And more bitter;
When you are away.
And I'm all yours;
Each and every one of your
Days and nights.

You have no idea how much I adore you,
You have no idea how much I love you,
I want and desire you,
I love you.

Yo te amo.

74 - The city:

Past fields of greenest sheer,
Grasses wet from high cloud tears.
Landscapes vast and abundantly free,
Brown leaves drop, littering the ground by trees.

Bordering boulders around to see,
Jagged and treacherous beyond those trees.
Further still the end of green,
Stands a less than natural scene.

Grey material, hard as rock,
Standing upon each other in blocks.
To prevent escape to all who dwell,
In this concrete, unnatural hell.

A standing fortress in beautiful land,
One species living, unwillingly crammed.
Slowly taking from abundancy,
Receding nature, until no longer seen.

Not only do these walls that stand;
Prevent escape to natural land.
Also stop entrance of nature from which we take,
A symbol to this world which we so hate.

75 - The wheelchair:
The prison I'm held in, seated and still,
Upon my wheelchair,
But it's so comfortable,
I can't be bothered to move.

Looking out of the windows near,
Everything seems so desolate and queer,
Leaves falling and crushing into the ground,
By their own weight, like me, spiralling down.

I'm just too lazy,
To look for my suicide.
It's coming to me anyway,
With the fake, pale smiles.

The arms I have hurt from broken veins,
Hiding snakes with pierced holes.
The eyes I have sting from lack of sleep,
And here comes my suicide.

She's dressed in white and
Adorned in small mouth movements.
I can't listen, I don't want to,
She breaks the snakes again, and again.

76 - To say:

A coin drops down,
Sinking into the well.
Sparking, a child-like frown.
An anxiety that nothing could quell,
Walking away as it continually fell.

The thought struck me as I walked,
An overwhelming urge to talk;
No king nor god will come,
Of that I am pessimistically sure
To rescue you from your slum,
Nor erase this pain you endure.

No matter the words I want to say,
I continue and forget my plan to take you away.
I wish to be in your presence,
To speak and tell you what I want.
To confess the love of a peasant,
And speak the words my heart can't.

"I came all this way to say;
I am here to take you away.
A hand to give and make yours,
Excuse me, for I am flawed.
No prince nor god am I,
The one who dies with every tear you cry.
Just a man, here I stand.
Waiting for you to take my hand."

77 - When I compare to a rose:
The perfect face delicately angled.
The lips so soft and kissable,
Like red leaves entangled.

And that adorable button nose that begs for a kiss.
That faint smell of sweetness, subtle and easy to miss.

The solid, strong, gorgeous eyes.
The lovely, touchable and cute cheeks,
Red, like bitten thighs.

And the beautiful, long and stroke-able hair.
The Roses next to you look so ugly and unfair.

The smooth chin that needs a delicate finger placed,
To stroke while it tilts it for a kiss leaving hint of my taste.
Your silky soft neck that makes my finger tips desire to trace.

The forehead for which a small kiss shall adorn,
To show how it is you I adore.

Oh there stands roses next to you?
Your beauty stands strong, while their's are few.

78 - Both as one:
Although your days are ended,
I still have a few more.
And I'm still here,
Decrepit and useless.

Death really means nothing more
Than losing the fire in your eyes.

So here we lay,
Our bodies in each other's way
Sharing a shallow grave.
Because when one goes,
So does the other.

Death really means nothing anymore,
Than losing the fire in my eyes.

So here we lay,
Two in the same grave.
I gave my life away,
And my body is here to stay.

79 - Silence:

We have been looking for something for awhile.
Beauty sitting under a delicate crown.
Life has a way of hiding its smile.
Leaving only your frown.
Death always not too far away,
Mortality here to stay.

Although through rolling mountains sorrow comes descending.
Pouring rain blurring what you once could see.
To break the clouds,
Is not a chance or blind luck.
Nor does fate owe any change,
To clear your heart
Of mountainous brutalities range.

In this world we found ruin.
Bodies covered in frost.
Never to be freshly renewed again.
You're lost,
Screaming loud in a
Deaf world.

80 - The realistic offer:

What is it that reality offers,
When people beg towards the sky?
Will it offer to me,
Something which I can see,
Without opening an eye?

What will come your way and what you want,
Isn't always viewable from your front.
Reality can be rather blunt,
What most need is:
A sharp love to help bear the brunt.

So what you look for is true romance?
But listen not to your heart,
Don't give it the chance.
What your brain chooses to love,
Will make you fear what's above.

A person to tell me when I'm corrupt,
To see a monster and still be able to look.
A person to respect and be loyal,
During and until the end of life's trial.

I don't own you,
And you don't own me.
Freely love and spend it on you.
I give my time to share with me,
Limited time and experience we spend,
I select you,
My love and my friend.

81 - Crave:
Love is a gift that is said to be gave,
To demand of us all which we crave,
Fiery passion is love's way,
Making us live and value this day.

Impatience is another of its traits,
The heart always feels it cannot wait,
For the love, which will intoxicate,
All that comes,
And what will come to be,
It is not love,
That claims all it can see.

82 - The leprosy:
The flesh losing its ability to hold,
Tears and falls into disgusting folds,
The pain felt by such a disease: Untold.
Leprosy comes and rips at the soul.

Evil; Corrupting and taking the skin,
Burying deeper and eating the liquid within.
Drying: with anguish the crying eyes,
Breaking down the inside's ties.

While in agony they grind their teeth,
No longer needing the help of priests.
It doesn't matter, they hold to their beliefs,
Because soon, they'll be deceased.

83 - The hermit:
In the furthest reaches of this cavernous beach,
Secluded and deluded sits a man with callused feet,
Alone and torn, yet why stay sat upon this lonely throne?:
To atone? Or merely to moan and groan while living alone?
No one will know, why his face he will not show.
Although our opinion we do not share,
We all know that neither of us care.

84 - Cycle:
Falling from the tree,
The seed plants itself underneath thee.
Taking the rain and shine,
Growing to cover the sky and blind.
Branching out and touching others,
This life now becomes the Mother.
This life now becomes the Father.
Branching out and touching others,
Growing to cover the sky and blind.
Taking the rain and shine,
The seed plants itself underneath thee,
Falling from the tree.

85 - Type of man:
He's the type of man,
Says he loves but never can;
Living with no plan.

86 - Empty house:
Empty and left house,
To fill the Summer Season;
Bringing new to old.

87 - Marx of history:[3]
The scarred Marks forever never leaving,
Break your back for a little loaf of bread.
Our nature: The greed; Always deceiving,
With change: To freedom we can be led.
Letting the working class love their chains,
The upper class decorate them with flowers,
Pick and throw them; Exorcize the *Specters*.
Who is the man telling us that we can,
Separate us from our passions and creations?
All in order only to further their plan.
Cull the flower; Embrace liberation.
Time to change, educate and use our brains.
Empty work keeping us in poverty.
Alienation; Making us a commodity.

---

[3] Karl Marx (1818-1883).

88 - Percy's romance:[4]

You're the most beautiful Shelley on my beach,
Towards you, my heart does reach.
The mask of anarchy crumbles to reveal your true face,
And I pick up your pieces with effortless grace.
Prometheus chained like our loving embrace.
The only thing to match the elegance of our entwined fate:
Dancing in circles, lost in trance.
We step deeper into our enduring romance.

---

[4] Percy Bysshe Shelley (1792-1822)

89 - Dreams be Dunn:[5]

Stood at the window I see my reflection,
No longer the nightgown do I wear.
Now Summer has come the frost has gone.
The corporeal fell away but still I am here.
My love has stayed and completed my transition,
From flesh to spirit, the other me sleeps like stone.

---

[5] A continuation of Douglas Dunn's (1942) poem *France*.

<u>90 - Eyes to see:</u>
O fair lady, so fresh and fine.
Lips none the sweeter.
I couldn't of chosen better,
When I made you mine.
Betwixt her fingers is the place for me,
So never the trouble approaches me.
To put my hand and hold her tight,
That face so fine, the smile inducing sight.

And is it not love that makes one blind?
So take and pluck out thine eyes,
Because you have no need to see.
Or of another person that you wish you could find,
It's not the heart that loves and sighs,
In order for you to be.

91 - Anti-life:

Life is often said;
To supply for those who try,
To feed those who into poverty bred,
To alleviate the baby's cry,
Place a smile upon the newlywed,
To kill the evil who against good defy,
But not the moral instead.
So I ask you; Who are those not fed?

Are the poor the victims of life?
Woe to them living amongst strife?
Now say you that they truly deserve
No empathy because that would be absurd?
No! Woe to you, the living instead,
Because you steal from all and mould life's bread.

92 - The dog's bite:
O, I am alive with eyes wide open,
Or maybe near death and to life groping.
Why a tanned angel? O Angel deliver me please.
I beg thee, take me under thy arms of faith and into thine sleeves.
And send me to my heart's content, to her if shy lays above.
The destiny that they can behold and hold for life until end with love.

"Fragile little heart I kiss with my lips,
But your body more fragile but beauty it retains.
And with you, I can always remain,
Without effort, because your love holds me within its grips."

O shush thou your little sweet lips,
And hold your fate's weight upon thy hips,
Now give me your taste so sweet,
And let me adore you upon thine heart's seat.

"No, I'm not the one who is perfect,
My love for you is just a human's.
I wish to take you and hold your hand.
And live happy and dreams of erotic."

O I tell you that you're not for me,
For you are your own and will forever be,
Not the type that costs a deed or fee,
But I love you as you, for as long as can be.

"Sunshine smile lighten up my day,
Your face, your cheeks, plumb and happy as can be.
A pleasure, to see and sings my heart as they so see.
Although not close but in my heart never far away."

O fair lady your strong eyes are mine,
Brown and strong like Tiger's lines,
To not love you would be a mortal crime.
Maybe not forever but I will give you my limited time.

"I hope you know that my passion, is destined to be yours.
I wish that you can hold it, like a dog that locks its jaws.

Although we may separate with each other, with sleep or distance leave,
It's not that my heart has gone anywhere, but in unison with you it breathes."

<u>93 - Repeated lines:</u>
And so it begins afresh,
Once again we hit on a nerve.
Taking what you feel you deserve.
Take apart your heart to undress.
Requiring of me that infinite test.
Thinking that we have something new,
With billions we feel among the few.
Leave your thoughts and put them to rest.

Like everything else, we are doomed by flux,
So allow me to use you as life's crutch.
Until death this will be the countless time.
And yet for me;
I have merely
Reached my repeated line.

94 - That which is due:

So what is it that I cry for:
When sorrow I know is due.
It's okay, I wipe away the tears,
Because I cry for you.
Then what is it that's so upsetting:
When depression comes not due.
It's not okay, I can't wipe away,
Because there's no reason to.

So when people say:
"It's okay to cry today,
But when tomorrow comes be sure
To smile that frown away."
But alas, that is the reason why:
I cry, and sigh, because depression doesn't die.

95 - The cold bed:
I wake to see you have rolled away.
You sleep with your face pressing the quilt's folds,
I stare at you through sore eyes and let you stay
Lying there, so still and so clearly cold,
And living with what we have been told.

Something, that one thing, scares me.
I love what lies inside you,
But hate what lives there too.
Wanting not to live as I, but as we.

I sneak up close beside you in bed,
To stroke and hold your balded head.
I embrace you in my warm living arms,
Kissing your forehead to wake you instead,
And lay with your body, silent and so calm.

96 - The face:

If you hold up the mirror,
Make it your face so I can see me.
My eyes beg at the sight, itching with curiosity
While the flesh beneath festers.

It feels I have all the time
To find how and why this face
Is mine.

Finger tips to touch the cold surface,
But never quite reach the angles,
To explore, to discover, to know the face too.

When I hold the mirror up for
You to see your face:
Do you see mine or your own?
Is it the face of tragedy,
Bleeding tears of mockery?
Is it your own identity,
You project on me?
Or is it two mirrors,
Seeing each other?

97 - A stranger to me:

He spoke to the stranger,
Not the passer by,
But himself.

I've never met you,
Nor known me,
For a second split.

I hear your voice,
After the thought,
It sounds the same.

So he thinks,
For all his life,
That those similar,
Are himself.
Are the same.

98 - The serpent of light:

Coiled, recoiled, spiralled into the night.
In rest, laid undressed.
Here lays the serpent of light.

Looking upon the body that causes me to transgress.
Wrapped in silk, heart in darkness: sly,
You think by luck angels have refused me trespass.

By the luck that decrees that you die,
Is it by the same that I stay in my hatred and pride?
Taking life to the sound of your suffocated sigh.

I take and squeeze that pathetic worm.
To return you to night.
Strangle and throttle the light and Orm.

You open wide, to try and find
Your air, your voice to cry
Out and scream. Opened so wide.

In this world, no matter how you try
You earn what you make happen, repress
Your efforts and cut your ties.

Luck plays no part in throttling to undress.
Taking the life's gown and light,
To clothe you in nightly death's dress.

99 - Ode to Wales:
In soft pastures, and on top of mountain trails.
Again, I return to the land of Cymru vales.
The land to make hearty and hale.
Mist cover the cottages on the hill of Treharris.
Green, vale, and life to bring
Creatures, young and brought with Spring.
Hear the baas and bleating, the lambs that sing,
In their fields which is their chalice.
Fossils to find amongst slate in Monknash,
Taking my time, growing slow, a child's time to pass.
A hammer to take, and open and smash,
Childhood adventures in the land of Wales.

100 - The sin of solitude:
So, I continue to be alone
Because of apparent sins that I won't atone.
Said myself like Satan once spoke:
Is it by my vanity that I be alone?
Is it such a crime to grow and live apart?
From the velvet chains I've broke,
This family-head I wish to be no part.

Acknowledgments:

I would like to firstly acknowledge all of the help with my ideas and life that was given to me by Samantha Peraza Ramírez.

Secondly I would like to thank everyone who has waited for this book and been patient with the delay in my first publication. Thank you.

Author's note:

All written work by Marcus Skjøte.

For personal contact of the author:
E-mail: solsilence@live.co.uk
Facebook: https://www.facebook.com/Solilska

My writing page:
https://www.facebook.com/MarcusSolilska
DeviantART: www.solilska.deviantart.com

All books can be found on:
lulu.com

Life is the one play with no script.

Printed in Great Britain
by Amazon